Christmas Quilting

20 Decorative Projects

by

Terry Thompson Evans

DOVER PUBLICATIONS, INC.

New York

Many thanks to Irlene Withroder
for her help in making the items
shown on the covers.

For information on ordering Templastic® (see page 4)
and a catalog of additional patterns, please send $2.00 to:

Peace Creek Farm
Rt. 1, Box 80
Sylvia, Kansas 67581

Published in Canada by General Publishing Company, Ltd.,
30 Lesmill Road, Don Mills, Toronto, Ontario.
Published in the United Kingdom by Constable and Company, Ltd.,
10 Orange Street, London WC2H 7EG.

Christmas Quilting: 20 Decorative Projects is a new work, first
published by Dover Publications, Inc., in 1988.

Manufactured in the United States of America
Dover Publications, Inc.
31 East 2nd Street
Mineola, N.Y. 11501

Library of Congress Cataloging-in-Publication Data

Evans, Terry Thompson.
    Christmas quilting : 20 decorative projects / by Terry Thompson
Evans.
        p.   cm.
    ISBN 0-486-25755-X
    1. Quilting—Patterns. 2. Christmas decorations. I. Title.
TT835.E93 1988
746.46—dc19   88-10842
                                                             CIP

Introduction

"Home for Christmas" is one of the great American traditions. Trimming the tree, hanging the stockings and decorating the house are important elements in this family- and home-oriented holiday. What better way is there to celebrate this tradition-filled season than with another great American tradition, quilting?

Here are twenty Christmas projects to brighten your home. Trim your tree with miniature quilt patches or hang a wreath on the front door to wish all who enter a Merry Christmas. Handmade stockings are sure to win Santa's approval, and a beautiful quilt to hang on a wall will add the finishing touch to your holiday decorations.

I hope that you enjoy making these decorations as much as I enjoyed designing them for you, and if I have helped you to start your own Christmas tradition, so much the better.

Merry Quilting!

General Instructions

Fabrics

Choose fabrics that are soft and closely woven enough so that they do not fray easily; however, do not use a fabric that is so closely woven that you will have trouble pushing the needle through it. Although 100% cotton is the easiest fabric to work with, cotton/polyester blends can be used. Avoid using fabrics that contain more than 30% polyester.

Before cutting your fabrics, wash them in hot water to preshrink them and to remove sizing and excess dye. Dry the fabrics and press them. Check the grainline of the fabric: lengthwise threads should be parallel to the selvage and crosswise threads exactly perpendicular to the selvage *(Fig. 1)*. If the fabric is off-grain, pull it gently on the bias in the opposite direction to the off-grain edge to straighten it *(Fig. 2)*.

The yardages given in the individual instructions are for 44"–45"-wide fabric.

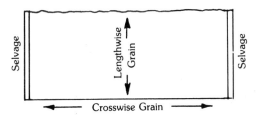

Fig. 1. Lengthwise threads should be parallel to the selvage and crosswise threads perpendicular to the selvage.

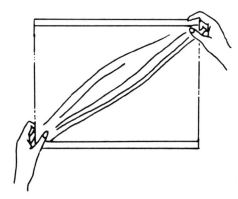

Fig. 2. Pull fabric on the true bias in the opposite direction to the off-grain edge to straighten fabric.

Making Templates

With the exception of a few large pieces, all of the templates for making the projects in this book are printed, full-size, on heavy card stock in the template section at the back of the book. Locate the templates you need and cut them apart, leaving some blank space around each template. With rubber cement, glue the templates to lightweight cardboard such as poster board. With an X-ACTO knife, carefully cut along the printed lines. Use sandpaper to smooth any rough edges. Some templates are too large to fit on one page and are divided into several parts. To use these templates, cut out all of the parts, cutting precisely on the joining lines. Tape the pieces together, matching the small numbers. Glue the joined templates to cardboard.

To make more permanent templates, place a sheet of transparent plastic such as Templastic® over the printed template and trace. Cut out the plastic template.

Cutting the Pieces

The templates are the size the patches will be after they are sewn; they do not include the ¼″ seam allowance.

To trace the templates to the fabric, lay the fabric on the work surface with the wrong side up. Place the template on the fabric near the top left edge (not on the selvage). If the template has an arrow printed on it, place the template so that this arrow is parallel or perpendicular to the selvage; if there is no arrow, place the template so that as many straight edges as possible are parallel to the lengthwise and crosswise grain *(Fig. 3)*.

Trace around the cardboard with a well-sharpened hard lead pencil. Use a dark pencil for light-colored fabrics and a light-colored pencil for dark fabrics. Hold the pencil at an angle as you trace so that the point is right against the edge of the template and so that it does not drag on the fabric. The line you draw will be the sewing line. Measure ¼″ around the shape and draw the cutting line *(Fig. 4)*. Continue moving

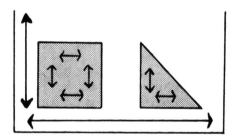

Fig. 3. Place templates on the fabric so that as many straight sides of the pattern as possible are parallel to the crosswise and lengthwise grain of the fabric.

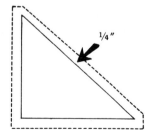

Fig. 4. The broken line is the cutting line. The solid line is the seam line; match to the line on the next patch. Sewing is done on the solid line.

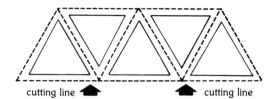

Fig. 5. The pieces can share a common cutting line.

and tracing the template, adding the seam allowance before going on to the next piece. You can save fabric by having the pieces share a common cutting line *(Fig. 5)*.

Two of the templates give only part of the finished pattern—one shows one quarter, while the other shows one half. To use these templates, mark center lines on the fabric. Matching the center lines of the template to those on the fabric, trace the template. Pivot the template, matching the center lines, and trace again. Continue in this way until the pattern is complete.

Certain shapes, particularly squares and triangles, can be effectively cut with a rotary cutter. Fold the fabric in half lengthwise, then trace *half* of the number of pieces needed to the fabric, having them share common cutting lines. Using the rotary cutter and a metal or heavy plastic ruler, cut along the longest cutting lines to form strips, then cut across the strips to form the individual pieces. With practice, four or more layers of fabric can be cut at one time.

Patterns for appliqué should be traced to the *right* side of the fabric. Because the seam allowance in appliqué does not have to be exact, it is not necessary to draw the cutting line onto the fabric; just leave about ½″ between pieces when tracing. Cut out the pieces, cutting approximately ¼″ outside the traced line. While the seam allowance on appliqué should never be more than ¼″, you may find it easier to work with a slightly smaller seam allowance.

If you have several different shapes to cut from one fabric, cut the larger ones first to avoid wasting fabric.

Sewing the Pieces Together

Patchwork can be done by hand or on the sewing machine. Machine piecing works well for projects with fairly large patches and straight seams, but on items where the individual patches are very small, or where pieces must be set into an angle, it is often easier to sew the patches together by hand.

To sew two patches together by hand, place them with right sides together. Place a pin through both pieces at each end of the pencil line; check on the back to make sure that the pins are exactly on the line *(Fig 6)*. Insert the needle at one end of the pencil line, securing it with a few backstitches. Sew along the line

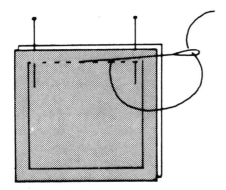

Fig. 6. Place a pin through both pieces at each end of the pencil line.

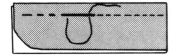

Fig. 7. Running stitch.

with small running stitches *(Fig. 7)*; if the seam is a long one, take a backstitch several places along the seam. Do not stitch beyond the end of the pencil line. Fasten the thread with several backstitches.

To sew the patches by machine, pin them together as described above. The presser foot on many sewing machines is exactly ¼″ wide, and can be used as a stitching guide. If the presser foot is not ¼″ wide, place a strip of masking tape ¼″ from the needle and use this as a guide. Using a stitch length of 8 to 10 stitches per inch, stitch the seam, securing the ends with back-stitching.

If you sew the pieces together by machine, you can save time by "chain sewing" the units. To do this, pin the patches together in pairs, and feed them through the machine without backstitching or clipping the threads at the end of each seam *(Fig. 8)*. Allow about 1″ between the units. When all the units are sewn, cut them apart. In chain sewing, you will stitch past the pencil line into the corners; however, unless the pieces are to be set into an angle this does not matter. If necessary, it is a simple matter to unravel the seam back to the end of the pencil line and tie off the threads.

Whether you sew the pieces together by hand or machine, always press the seam before crossing it with another seam. Press seams to one side, toward the darker fabric whenever possible.

When you are joining rows of previously joined patches, be very careful that the seam lines of the patches match exactly.

Fig. 8. Chain sewing small units.

Occasionally, it will be necessary to sew a patch into an angle. To do this by hand, pin the first side in place; take a backstitch exactly at the corner and sew to the end of the seam. Pin the second side in place and, once again, sew from the corner to the end of the seam. To sew an angle on the machine, pin the first side in place and stitch from the end of the seam to the corner, ending with the needle in the fabric exactly at the corner. Lift the presser foot and pivot the fabric. Lower the presser foot and continue sewing, pulling the excess fabric out of the way.

To join two curved pieces, clip the seam allowance of the concave edge every ¼″ to ⅜″ *(Fig. 9)*. Pin the pieces together and sew.

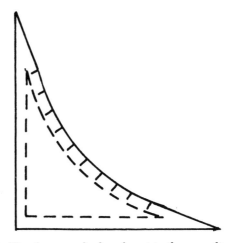

Fig. 9. Clip the curved edge almost to the seam line.

How to Appliqué

Appliqué consists of sewing a fabric shape onto a fabric background. Although it can be done by machine, the projects in this book were worked by hand and this is the method described here.

Cut out the appliqué pieces as described above. If the shape is a complex one with many curves and corners, or if you are a beginner at appliqué, you will probably find it easier to turn under and baste the seam allowance of the piece before pinning it to the background. If the edge of the appliqué patch is curved, clip the seam allowance almost to the stitching line in several places. Fabrics that are 100% cotton have more "give" than cotton blends, and will consequently need less clipping. Thread a needle with a contrasting color of thread and make a knot in the end. Working from the right side of the patch, baste around the edge of the piece, turning the seam allowance to the wrong side so that the pencil line does not show. For simple shapes, you may find it easier not to baste the seam allowance in advance, but to turn it under with the point of your needle as you sew.

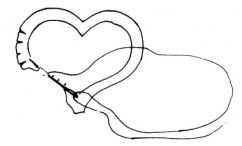

Fig. 10. Attaching an appliqué to the background with blindstitch.

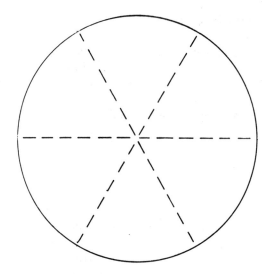

Fig. 12. Basting a circular piece.

Pin the appliqué to the background. Thread the needle with matching thread and knot the end. Bring the needle through the background fabric from the back, very close to the edge of the appliqué. Sew the appliqué in place with a blindstitch, sewing right along the folded edge of the appliqué *(Fig. 10)*. The stitches should be almost invisible from the right side of the fabric. Pull the stitches tight enough to hold the appliqué firmly against the background, but not so tight that the fabric puckers. Be very careful to sew points and corners down securely. Fasten the thread with a few backstitches on the wrong side of the background and cut the thread. Remove the basting.

Preparing to Quilt

Three of the projects, the Christmas Star Quilt, the Christmas Tree Wall Quilt and the Log Cabin Tree Skirt, are finished by layering the decorated top, quilt batting and a lining, then quilting them and binding the edges.

Cut the lining about 4″ larger all around than the completed top, joining lengths of fabric to make the lining, if necessary. (If you plan to quilt the Log Cabin Tree Skirt in a frame, cut the lining square rather than

round.) Cut the batting slightly smaller than the lining. Spread the lining, wrong side up, on the work surface. Center the batting over it, smoothing out any wrinkles. Place the decorated top, right side up, on the batting. Beginning in the center of the quilt and taking very long stitches, baste to the midpoint of each side and to each of the four corners *(Fig. 11)*. To baste a circular piece, baste from the center to the edge, dividing the circle into several sections *(Fig. 12)*. Baste around the outer edges.

Traditionally, a quilt was mounted in a large floor frame that held the layers taut as the fabric was quilted. Today many quilters use a hoop rather than a frame, and still others quilt without either. Whether to use a frame, a hoop or nothing at all is a matter of personal preference.

Because these projects are fairly small, a full-size frame can easily be made from artist's stretcher strips. Buy two strips equal to the length of the quilt plus 5″ and two strips equal to the width plus 5″. Assemble the stretcher strips, wedging the corners tightly so that they do not shift. Center the quilt, right side up, over the frame. Attach one edge of the lining to the frame with thumbtacks or a staple gun. Pull the quilt taut and attach the opposite edge of the lining to the opposite stretcher strip. Attach the remaining edges in the same way. When quilting, balance the frame on the backs of four chairs.

If you decide not to use a frame, you may wish to add further rows of basting to hold the quilt layers together more securely.

If using a hoop, place it over the center of the quilt and pull the quilt taut, moving the excess fullness toward the edge. Begin quilting in the center and work out to the edges, moving the hoop as needed. In order to keep the quilt taut, you may need to use a smaller hoop as the work comes closer to the edge of the quilt.

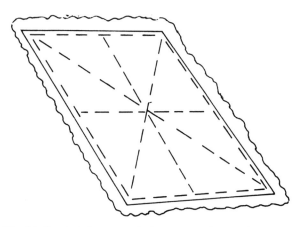

Fig. 11. Basting the top to the batting and lining, through the center and around the edges.

The Quilting Stitch

The quilting stitch is a simple running stitch worked through all three layers of the quilt. In addition to your basted quilt, you will need quilting needles (called "betweens"), thread made specially for quilting, or regular sewing thread coated with beeswax and a thimble. Even if you do not usually use a thimble for sewing, you should wear a thimble on the middle finger of your right hand for quilting. Some quilters also wear a thimble on the index finger of their left hand.

To begin, thread the needle with an 18″ length of thread; knot one end. Bring the needle from the lining to the top at the point where you wish to begin quilting. Tug gently, but firmly, on the thread until the knot "pops" through the lining and lodges in the batting. Now, place your left hand under the quilt and your right hand on top. Insert the needle into the quilt at a 45° angle and push it through with the thimble until you feel the point with your left index finger. Push the tip of the needle up with the left index finger, while pressing the eye of the needle flat against the quilt top with the thimble. Push the needle through to the front with the right hand. Repeat this process for each stitch. Try to get several stitches on the needle before pulling it all the way through the fabric.

Although the ideal in quilting is to have very small stitches, it is more important that the stitches all be the same length. With practice, you will be able to make smaller stitches. Also, the shorter the needle, the smaller the stitches, so always work with the shortest needle you can comfortably handle.

End the line of quilting by making a single back-stitch, then running the thread into the batting. Bring the needle through the lining to the back and cut the thread close to the surface of the lining. Take the quilt out of the frame or hoop and remove the basting stitches.

Small pieces can be quilted on the sewing machine, using a stitch length of 8 to 10 stitches per inch.

Binding the Quilt

Straight edges can be bound with either straight or bias binding; curved edges must be bound with bias binding. Cut the binding 2″ wide, joining strips until the binding is long enough to go around the edges of the quilt, plus 2″ to 3″. Turn the ends of the binding strip to the wrong side, then fold the strip in half lengthwise with the wrong side in.

Trim the edges of the quilt layers so that they are even, leaving ¼″ seam allowance all around the quilt. Pin the binding around the edges of the quilt on the right side, matching the raw edges and mitering the corners. Overlap the ends of the binding. Stitch around ¼″ from the edge. Fold the binding over the raw edge of the quilt and slip-stitch the folded edge to the lining.

Quilted Christmas Stockings

Approximately 19″ long

Materials for Basic Stocking

¾ yd. pre-quilted fabric
Fabrics for decorations
Sewing thread to match fabrics

To Make Basic Stocking

Trace two stockings to pre-quilted fabric, turning template over to trace second stocking. Add ¼″ seam allowance around stockings; cut out. Cut heel and toe appliqués and patches for decorations as indicated in the individual instructions.

Pin the heel and toe to the stocking front. Turn under the seam allowance on the inner edges of the heel and toe; appliqué in place. Baste the outer edges to the stocking. Decorate the stocking front.

Right sides together, pin the stocking front to the back. Stitch, leaving the top edge open. Turn the stocking right side out. Turn under and stitch ¼″ on the top edge. Fold a 1″-deep hem to the inside of the stocking and slip-stitch in place.

Cut a 2″ by 5″ strip of fabric to make a hanging loop. Fold the strip in half lengthwise with the right side in. Stitch the long raw edges and one end. Turn the strip right side out. Turn in the raw edges and slip-stitch them together. Bring the ends of the strip together to form a loop and pin the loop inside the stocking at the center back seam. Slip-stitch it securely in place.

Templates for the stockings appear on Plates 1, 2 and 3.

Fig. 1

HOLLY STOCKING

Materials

¾ yd. white pre-quilted fabric for stocking
Scraps of green calico and solid red fabric
Sewing thread to match fabrics

Number of Pieces to Cut

Stocking	2 from quilted fabric
Heel and Toe	1 each from green
Leaves	6 green
Berry	1 red

To Make

Appliqué the heel and toe to the stocking front. Arrange the leaves on the stocking front to form a circle *(Fig. 1)*, having the top of the circle about 3″ below the top edge of the stocking. Appliqué the leaves in place; appliqué the berry over the center of the circle.

Assemble the stocking, adding a white hanging loop.

PATCHWORK STOCKING #1 (pictured)

Materials

¾ yd. white pre-quilted fabric for stocking
Scraps red and black houndstooth check, green pin
   dot and solid white fabrics
Sewing thread to match fabrics

Number of Pieces to Cut

Stocking	2 from quilted fabric
Heel and Toe	1 each from red
Template A	8 green, 8 white
Template B	4 red, 1 white

To Make

Sew a green A triangle to the left-hand side of a white
A triangle to form a larger triangle *(Fig. 1)*. Repeat
with remaining A triangles. Sew two patched triangles
together along the diagonal edge to form a square
(Fig. 2). Repeat with the remaining triangles. Sew the
patched squares to the B squares as in *Fig. 3*, first
joining the squares together in horizontal rows, then
sewing the rows together.

   Turn under the raw edges of the block and appliqué
it to the stocking front about 3″ below the top edge.
Appliqué the heel and toe to the stocking front.

   Assemble the stocking, adding a white hanging
loop.

Fig. 1

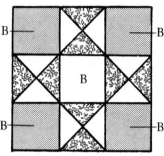

Fig. 2

Fig. 3

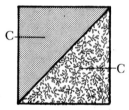

Fig. 1

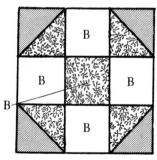

Fig. 2

PATCHWORK STOCKING #2

Materials

¾ yd. green pre-quilted calico for stocking
Scraps red calico and solid green, red and white
   fabrics
Threads to match fabric

Number of Pieces to Cut

Stocking	2 from quilted fabric
Heel and Toe	1 each from solid red
Template B	4 white, 1 solid green
Template C	4 solid green, 4 solid red

To Make

Sew the red C triangles to the green C triangles along
the diagonal edge to form squares *(Fig. 1)*. Sew the
patched squares and B squares together as in *Fig. 2*,
first joining the squares together in rows, then sewing
the rows together.

   Turn under the raw edges of the block and appliqué
it to the stocking front about 3″ below the top edge.
Appliqué the heel and toe to the stocking front.

   Assemble the stocking, adding a red hanging loop.

PATCHWORK STOCKING #3

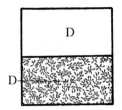

Fig. 1

Materials

¾ yd. solid red pre-quilted fabric for stocking
Scraps green calico and solid red and white fabrics
Threads to match fabrics

Number of Pieces to Cut

Stocking	2 from quilted fabric
Heel and Toe	1 each from white
Template B	1 red
Template C	4 red, 4 green calico
Template D	4 green calico, 4 white

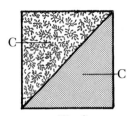

Fig. 2

To Make

Sew the green D rectangles to the white D rectangles along the long edge to form squares *(Fig. 1)*. Sew the red C triangles to the green C triangles along the diagonal edge to form squares *(Fig. 2)*. Sew the patched squares and B squares together as in *Fig. 3*, first joining the squares together in rows, then sewing the rows together.

Turn under the raw edges of the block and appliqué it to the stocking front about 3″ below the top edge. Appliqué the heel and toe to the stocking front.

Assemble the stocking, adding a white hanging loop.

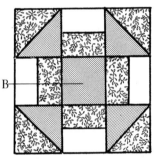

Fig. 3

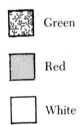

Green

Red

White

11

Christmas Tree Wall Quilt

Approximately 33½" by 46"

Materials

1½ yds. green calico for lining and binding
1½ yds. solid medium green fabric
¼ yd. each 4 different red and 4 different green calicoes
Scraps of solid dark green and solid red fabric
36" by 48" piece of quilt batting
Green, red and white sewing thread
Green quilting thread

Number of Pieces to Cut

Template A	26 assorted red calicoes, 23 assorted green calicoes
Template B	2 solid dark green
Template C	2 solid dark green
Template D	5 solid red
Template E	1 solid dark green
Template F	10 assorted red calicoes, 10 assorted green calicoes

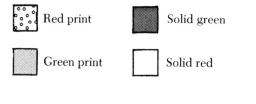

Red print   Solid green

Green print   Solid red

To Make

Sew A patches together to form the tree as follows: Beginning at the top of the tree with a red patch and alternating red and green calicoes, sew nine patches together to form a diagonal row *(Fig. 1)*. For the second row, begin with green and sew eight patches together as before. The third row begins with red and contains seven patches. Rows 4, 5 and 6 each contain six patches; rows 4 and 6 begin with green and row 5 begins with red. Row 7 begins with red and contains three patches; row 8 begins with green and contains two patches; row 9 consists of a single red patch. Sew the rows together following *Fig. 2*.

To make the tree trunk, sew a B patch to the right-hand side of the bottom red point of the tree *(Fig. 3)*. Sew the other B patch and the C patches to the remaining green A patch *(Fig. 4)*; sew this piece to the tree to complete the trunk *(Fig. 5)*.

From medium green, cut the background 33½" by 40½". Fold the background in half vertically and crease to mark the center. Pin the tree to the background, centering it and having the lower edge about 1" above the edge of the background. Appliqué the tree in place.

Following *Fig. 6*, sew the red star points *(Template D)* around the green star center *(Template E)*; appliqué the star to the top of the tree.

Using a very sharp #2 lead pencil, lightly trace twelve snowflakes (two of each design) to the background. There are two ways of tracing the snowflakes to the fabric. For the first method, remove the pages

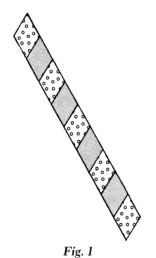

Fig. 1

containing the snowflake patterns from the book and place them on the work surface. Place the fabric over the pattern and trace it directly. For the second method, cut out the snowflake templates and place them on the right side of the fabric. Trace around the templates.

Using a ruler or yardstick, lightly draw a straight line along the left-hand edge of the tree, ending the line at the center at the top and extending the line to the edge of the background at the bottom. Skip over the snowflakes when you come to them. Draw additional lines parallel to the first and 1¼″ apart until the left-hand side of the background is completely filled with parallel lines. Draw lines slanting in the opposite direction on the right-hand side of the background; the lines should meet in a V at the center.

Sew ten F patches together to form a strip. Sew this strip to the top of the hanging; trim the ends of the strip even with the edges of the hanging. Sew the remaining F patches together and sew them to the bottom of the hanging.

Cut the lining 38″ by 50″. Assemble the lining, batting and hanging. Quilt along the seam lines of the tree and star patches and around the outer edge of the tree and star; quilt along all pencil lines. Quilting the borders is optional.

Bind the hanging, mitering the corners.

Fig. 2

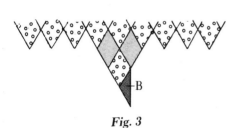

Fig. 3

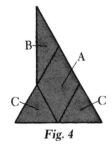

Fig. 4

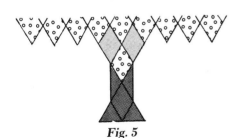

Fig. 5

Fig. 6

Templates for this quilt appear on Plates 4, 5 and 6.

13

Log Cabin Tree Skirt

Approximately 42″ in diameter

Materials

1¾ yds. dark green calico for lining and binding
¾ yd. each solid red and solid dark green fabrics
⅛ yd. each sixteen different calicoes for log cabin
    blocks: 4 light red (fabrics R1–R4), 4 dark red
    (fabrics R5–R8), light green (fabrics G1–G4) and
    dark green (fabrics G5–G8)
45″ square of quilt batting
Red sewing thread
Red quilting thread

Number of Pieces to Cut

Template A	3 solid red, 3 solid green
Template B	3 R1, 3 G1
Template C	3 R1, 3 R5, 3 G1, 3 G5
Template D	3 R2, 3 R5, 3 G2, 3 G5
Template E	3 R2, 3 R6, 3 G2, 3 G6
Template F	3 R3, 3 R6, 3 G3, 3 G6
Template G	3 R3, 3 R7, 3 G3, 3 G7
Template H	3 R4, 3 R7, 3 G4, 3 G7
Template I	3 R4, 3 R8, 3 G4, 3 G8
Template J	3 R8, 3 G8
Template K	3 solid red, 3 solid green
Template K reversed	3 solid red, 3 solid green
Template L	3 solid red, 3 solid green
Template L reversed	3 solid red, 3 solid green

Fig. 1

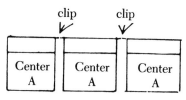

Fig. 2

Fig. 3

To Make

This tree skirt is made up of six log cabin blocks—3 red and 3 green. Wedges (*Templates K and L*) of the contrasting color are sewn to the block to form one section of the skirt.

The skirt can easily be made on the sewing machine, and lends itself to "chain sewing" the blocks (see General Instructions).

Make the six blocks as follows: Pin the light-colored B strip to the left-hand edge of the A center square (*Fig. 1*). Repeat for each block. Stitch the patches together, without backstitching or clipping the threads at the end of each seam (*Fig. 2*). When all of the units are stitched, clip the threads between them. Press the seams to one side. Continuing to chain stitch in this manner, stitch the light C strip to the top of the first unit (*Fig. 3*). Stitch the dark C strip to the right-hand side (*Fig. 4*), then the dark D strip to the bottom (*Fig. 5*). Working clockwise, continue adding strips following *Fig. 6*. The letters in the diagram refer to the templates, the numbers refer to the fabrics. The finished block will be divided in half diagonally—one side being light and the other dark (*Fig. 7*).

Templates for this tree skirt appear on Plates 7, 8 and 9.

Fig. 4

Sew the K wedges to the dark edges of the block as in *Fig. 8* to form the outside edge of the section. Sew the L star points to the light edges of the block as in *Fig. 9*; sew the short straight edges of the points together above the block. This completes the section.

Arrange the sections to form a circle, alternating the colors. Sew the sections together leaving one edge unsewn.

Assemble the lining, batting and patched skirt; quilt along the seam lines of the sections, around the outer edge of each log cabin block and around each block two strips in from the outer edge. Bind the edges of the skirt.

Fig. 5

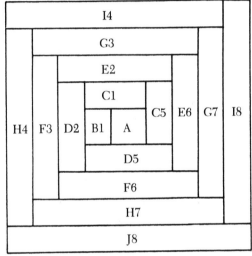

Fig. 6

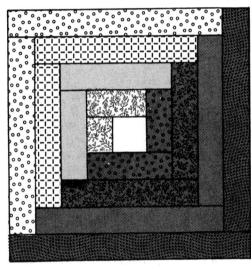

Fig. 7

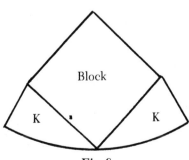

Fig. 8

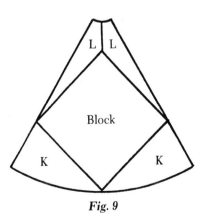

Fig. 9

Gathered Wreath

Approximately 16″ in diameter

Materials

¾ yd. each red and green calico
2½ yds. white rickrack
2½ yds. 2″-wide lace edging
12″ diameter rounded plastic foam wreath
Knife or hacksaw for cutting plastic foam
Glue for plastic foam
Thread to match fabrics

To Make

From each fabric, cut two 7¾″ by 44″ strips; trim off the selvages. Right sides together, stitch each pair of matching strips together along one short end.

Baste rickrack along one long edge of the red strip on the right side of the fabric, having the outer points of the rickrack just touching the cut edge of the fabric. Stitch along the center of the rickrack. Place the fabric strips with right sides in; stitch exactly on top of the previous stitching. Stitch ¼″ from the other long edge to form a tube; turn the tube right side out.

Working on the red side of the tube, mark a pencil line along the tube, 2¼″ from the edge with the rickrack. Pin the lace edging to the fabric, having the base of the heading along the pencil line and the lace pointing away from the edge. Stitch along the line, stopping 1″ from one end. Mark a second line 3⅜″ from the first; stitch, stopping 1″ from the end as before *(see Fig. 1)*. Press the lace over the stitching toward the edge of the tube.

Cut a 6″ section from the foam wreath *(Fig. 2)*. Slip the fabric tube over the larger section of the wreath with the lace on the outside. Glue the cut-out section of the wreath in place; allow to dry thoroughly. Distribute the fabric evenly around the wreath. Turn ½″ on the unstitched end of the tube to the wrong side of the fabric. Slip this end over the raw end of the tube and slip-stitch securely.

From each fabric, cut a 2½″ by 44″ strip. Place the strips with right sides together; trim the ends at a 45° angle *(Fig. 3)*. Stitch ¼″ from all edges, leaving a 3″ opening in the center of the long edge. Turn the strip right side out; turn in the edges of the opening and slip-stitch. With the green side out, tie the strip into a bow. Sew to the wreath as in the photograph.

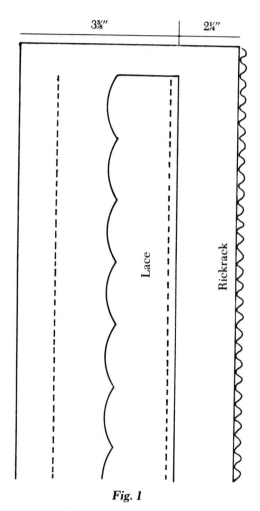

Fig. 1

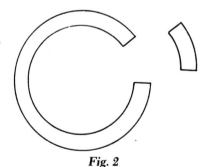

Fig. 3

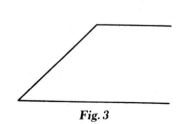

Fig. 2

Christmas Star Quilt

Approximately 46″ square

Materials

3 yds. fabric for lining
1¾ yds. cream fabric with green pin dots for borders and background
1½ yds. dark green calico
¾ yd. red calico
½ yd. solid green fabric for leaves and binding
48″ square of quilt batting
Sewing thread to match fabrics
White quilting thread

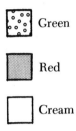

Green

Red

Cream

Number of Pieces to Cut

Template A	112 green calico, 132 red calico
Template B	12 green calico
Template C	8 cream, 4 green calico
Template D	4 cream
Template D reversed	4 cream
Template E	4 green calico
Template F	12 green calico
Template G	12 red calico
Template H	4 green calico (place template on fold when cutting)
Holly Leaf	24 solid green
Berry	8 solid red

From cream, cut 4 borders 9½″ by 46½″ (these dimensions include the seam allowances).

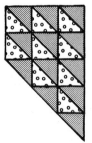

Fig. 1

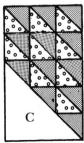

Fig. 2

To Make

Make pine tree block as follows: Sew nine green and twelve red A triangles together as in *Fig. 1,* first sewing the patches together in horizontal rows, then sewing the rows together. Sew a cream C triangle to the diagonal edge to form a rectangle *(Fig. 2).* Sew four green and three red A triangles together as in *Fig. 3* to form the roots of the tree. Sew D patches to each side of the E patch *(Fig. 4);* sew this piece to the roots, pivoting carefully at the corners. Sew a green C triangle to the diagonal edge of this piece to form a square *(Fig. 5).* Sew the patched square and the patched rectangle together as in *Fig. 6.* Sew A and B patches together following *Fig. 7;* sew a cream C patch to the diagonal edge to form a rectangle. Sew this piece to the previously joined pieces to form a 14½″ block *(Fig. 8).* Repeat to form a total of four pine tree blocks.

Arrange the pine tree blocks with the tops of the trees meeting; sew them together, carefully matching the seam lines on all patched pieces. The quilt top should now be 28½″ square.

Templates for this quilt appear on Plates 10, 11 and 12.

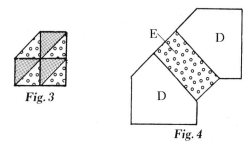

Fig. 3

Fig. 4

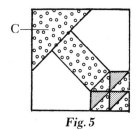

Fig. 5

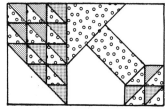

Fig. 6

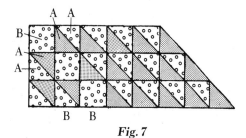

Fig. 7

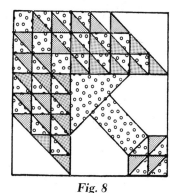

Fig. 8

Fold one of the borders in half crosswise and crease to mark the center. Unfold the piece and place it on the work surface, wrong side up, with the long edges at the top and bottom. With a pencil, mark a point 14″ to the right of the center and ¼″ below the top edge. Mark a second point 23″ to the right of the center and ¼″ above the lower edge. Draw a line connecting these two points *(Fig. 9)*; this will be the sewing line for mitering the corner. Trim the excess fabric 1″ outside the pencil line. Repeat on the left-hand side.

Turn the border right side up with the long edge at the bottom. Fold one of the green swag appliqués *(Template F)* in half to find the center. Matching the center lines, pin this patch to the border with the scalloped edge 2″ from the lower edge of the border. Add a green swag to either side of the first, allowing about ¼″ of space between them. Pin a red swag appliqué *(Template G)* to the top of each green swag. Arrange the holly leaves in groups of three on the border just above the meeting of the swags; place a berry at the base of each group of leaves. Refer to *Fig. 10* to check placement of appliqués. Sew the appliqués in place.

Mark and appliqué the remaining three borders in the same way.

Right sides together, pin a border to one edge of the quilt top, matching the center line of the border to the center seam of the top and having the edges of the top extend ¼″ past the pencil line on the border. Stitch the border in place, starting and stopping exactly on the pencil line. Repeat with the remaining borders. Right sides together, pin the corners of the borders together, matching the pencil lines. Stitch; trim seams to ¼″ and press them to one side.

Pin a corner appliqué *(Template H)* over each corner seam, having the bottom of the appliqué about 3½″ from the corner (measured along the corner seam). Appliqué in place.

Cut the lining fabric in half crosswise; cut one of the halves in half lengthwise. Trim the selvages from the pieces and sew the two narrow lengths to either side of the wider piece. Press the seams to one side.

Assemble the lining, batting and quilt top. Quilt around all of the appliqués, ⅛″ away. Quilt ⅛″ inside the seam lines of the green A triangles and ⅛″ outside the edge of the pine trees.

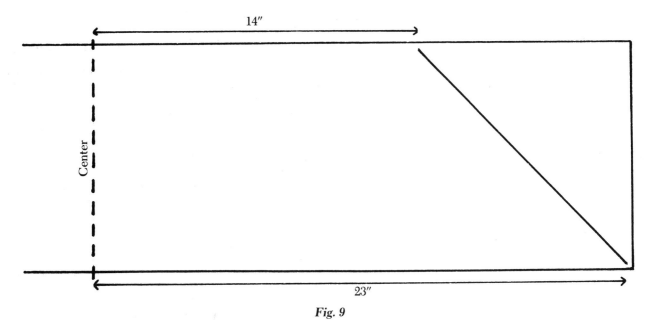

Fig. 9

Fig. 10

Holly Berry Wreath

Approximately 14″ in diameter

Materials

¾ yd. solid dark green fabric for wreath
¼ yd. each red calico and green calico for leaves
⅛ yd. solid red fabric for berries
45″ by 60″ crib size quilt batt
1 to 1½ lbs. polyester stuffing
Threads to match fabrics

Number of Pieces to Cut

Leaves   26 red calico, 26 green calico
Berries   18 to 20 solid red

From solid green, cut two 18″-diameter circles; cut a 4″-diameter circle from the center of each to form a wreath *(Fig. 1)*. These dimensions include ¼″ seam allowance.

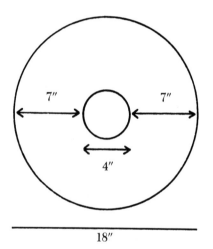

Fig. 1

Fig. 2

Fig. 3

To Make

Place green wreaths with right sides together. Stitch around ¼″ from outer edge. Clip seam allowance almost to stitching every 1″ to 1¼″; turn wreath right side out. Turn in ¼″ on edges of center opening. Pin the inner edges of the wreath together and begin to slip-stitch. When about half of the opening is sewn, begin stuffing the wreath firmly. Continue stuffing as you sew the remainder of the opening.

Baste batting to half of the green and half of the red leaves; trim the batting ¼″ smaller all around than the leaf. With the right sides together, pin the unbacked leaves to the backed leaves, matching the colors. Stitch around, leaving the short straight edge open. Clip the curved edges and turn the leaves right side out. Turn in the raw edges and slip-stitch. Machine-quilt along the broken lines indicated on the template.

To make the berries, thread a needle with red thread. Work a row of small running stitches around each berry, about ⅛″ from the edge *(Fig. 2)*, leaving about 3″ of thread at each end. Place a small amount of stuffing in the center of each circle, then draw up the gathers *(Fig. 3);* tie off the thread.

Arrange the leaves on the wreath as desired; tack them in place. Tack the berries to the leaves at random.

Templates for this wreath appear on Plate 13.

20

General Instructions for Christmas Tree Ornaments

These ornaments are miniature versions of traditional quilt patterns. The individual patches are very small, some of them no more than ½″ on a side, and must be handled carefully.

All of the ornaments are made from off-white muslin and solid red fabric; ½ yd. of each fabric, plus 1 yd. of muslin for the linings and a 45″ by 60″ crib-size quilt batt will make all eleven ornaments. In addition, the Primrose and Grandmother's Flower Garden ornaments use scraps of green fabric.

Trace the templates to the fabric and cut them out as described under "Making Templates" *(page 3)* and "Cutting the Pieces" *(page 4)*. Lay the pieces on a terry towel, arranging them following the diagrams and the photographs. Pin them to the towel so that they do not get lost.

Because the pieces are so small, hand piecing is recommended. The individual instructions suggest an order in which to sew the patches together. Sewing them in this order will eliminate setting pieces into an angle.

When the design is complete, cut the lining the same size and shape as the ornament. Unless otherwise directed, baste a layer of batting to the wrong side of the ornament; trim the batting ⅛″ smaller all around than the ornament. Pin the ornament to the lining with the right sides together. Stitch around ¼″ from the edge, leaving a small opening. Clip the corners and curves and turn the ornament right side out through the opening. Turn in the raw edges of the opening and slip-stitch them together. Quilt the piece as directed.

To make a hanging loop, cut a 1″ by 4″ strip of fabric. Fold the long raw edges to the center, then fold the strip in half lengthwise. Slip-stitch the folded edges together. Fold the strip in half to form a loop and tack the ends together. Tack the loop to the wrong side of the ornament. Decorative cord or narrow ribbon may also be used to make the loop.

Grandmother's Fan Ornament

Approximately 4″ high and 5″ wide

Materials

Red and off-white fabric
5″ square of quilt batting
Red and off-white sewing thread
Red quilting thread

Number of Pieces to Cut

Template A   2 red, 2 off-white
Template B   1 red

▨ Red   ☐ Off-white

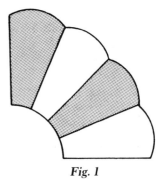

Fig. 1

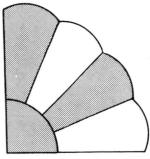

Fig. 2

To Make

Alternating colors, sew the fan sections *(Template A)* together along the long edges, stopping exactly on the seam lines *(Fig. 1)*. Pin the fan center *(Template B)* to the fan; stitch *(Fig. 2)*.

Assemble the fan, adding a hanging loop at the base. Quilt along the seam lines.

Templates for this ornament appear on Plate 15.

Schoolhouse Ornament

Approximately 3¾″ square

Materials

Red and off-white fabric
4″ square of quilt batting
Off-white sewing thread
Off-white quilting thread

■ Red

□ Off-white

Number of Pieces to Cut

Template A	2 red, 1 off-white
Template B	1 red
Template C	3 red, 2 off-white
Template D	1 red
Template E	1 red
Template F	1 off-white
Template G	1 off-white
Template H	1 red
Template I	2 red
Template J	1 off-white
Template K	1 off-white
Template K reversed	1 off-white

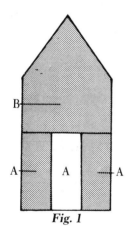

Fig. 1

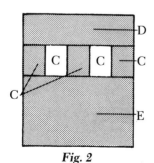

Fig. 2

To Make

Sew a red A patch to each long edge of the off-white A patch; sew the B patch to the top of this piece to form the house front *(Fig. 1)*. Alternating the colors, sew the five C patches together along the long edges to form a strip; sew the D patch to the top and the E patch to the bottom of the strip to form the house side *(Fig. 2)*. Sew the F strip to the left-hand edge of the house side *(Fig. 3)*. Sew the G patch to one diagonal edge of the H patch to form the roof *(Fig. 4)*, then sew the roof to the house side *(Fig. 5)*. Join the house side to the house front *(Fig. 6)*. Sew an I patch to either side of the J patch to form a strip; sew this to the top of the house. Finally, sew the K patches into the upper corners of the block, pivoting at the inner points *(Fig. 7)*.

Assemble the ornament; quilt along the seam lines of the off-white patches.

Templates for this ornament appear on Plate 13.

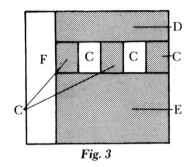

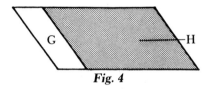

Fig. 3

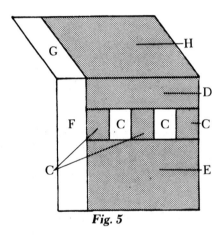

Fig. 4

Fig. 5

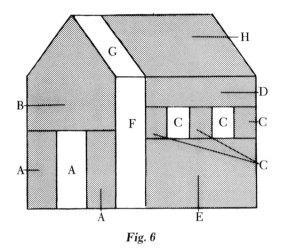

Fig. 6

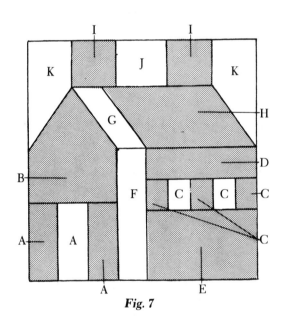

Fig. 7

23

Star Ornament

Approximately 4¾", point to point

Materials

Red and off-white fabric
5″ square of quilt batting
Off-white sewing thread
Off-white quilting thread

Number of Pieces to Cut

Diamond 4 red, 4 off-white

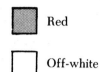

Red

Off-white

To Make

Sew a red and an off-white diamond together along one edge *(Fig. 1)*. Repeat with the remaining diamonds to form 4 pairs. Sew two of the pairs together to make a half-star *(Fig. 2)*; repeat with the remaining pairs. Sew the half-stars together—the diamonds should come to a point at the center *(Fig. 3)*.

Baste batting to the wrong side of the star; trim it ¼″ smaller all around than the star. Cut the lining the size and shape of the star. Turn under the seam allowances of both the star and the lining, trimming the points and clipping the corners as needed. Pin the star to the lining with the wrong sides in; slip-stitch them together. Quilt along the seam lines of the diamonds.

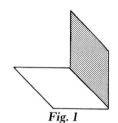

Fig. 1

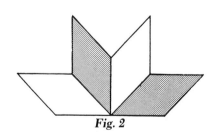

Fig. 2

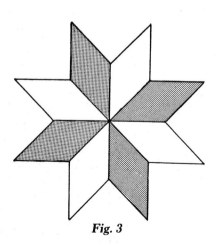

Fig. 3

The template for this ornament appears on Plate 14.

Grandmother's Flower Garden Ornament

Approximately 2½″ in diameter

Materials

Red, off-white and green fabric
Red sewing thread
Red quilting thread

Number of Pieces to Cut

Hexagon   6 red, 1 off-white

 Red

 Off-white

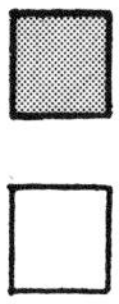

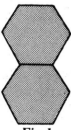

Fig. 1

To Make

Making sure that the grain of the fabric runs parallel to the seam, sew 2 red hexagons together *(Fig. 1)*. Repeat with 2 more red hexagons. Sew a red hexagon to opposite sides of the off-white hexagon, again being careful to have the fabric grain parallel to the seam *(Fig. 2)*. Carefully sew the two red strips to each side of the longer strip, pivoting at the corners and points *(Fig. 3)*.

Assemble the ornament, omitting batting. Attach a long green hanging loop. Quilt around the center hexagon.

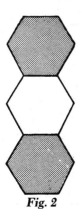

Fig. 2

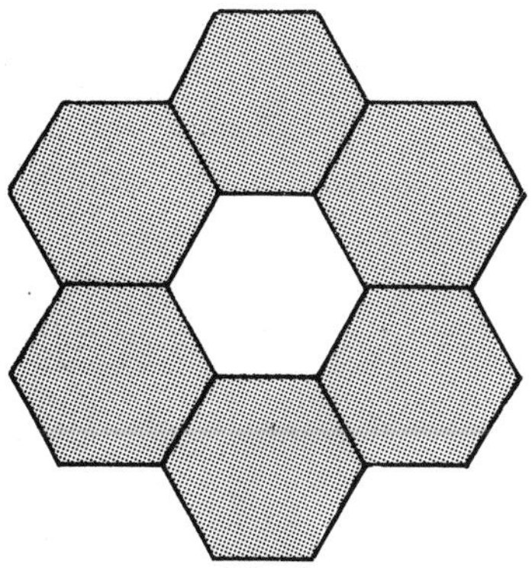

Fig. 3

The template for this ornament appears on Plate 14.

Primrose Ornament

Approximately 6½" in diameter

Materials

Red, off-white and green fabric
Yellow embroidery floss
5" square of quilt batting
Red, off-white and green sewing thread
Red quilting thread

Number of Pieces to Cut

Background	2 off-white
Wreath	1 green
Flower	4 red
Leaf	4 green

To Make

Fold one background circle in half, then half again; crease along folds to mark center. Repeat with wreath *(Fig. 1)*. Matching center lines, appliqué wreath to circle. On each flower, embroider five yellow French knots *(Fig. 2)*. Pin flowers to wreath, centering a flower over each crease. Arrange a leaf on the right-hand side of each flower along the outer edge of the wreath *(Fig. 3)*. Appliqué pieces in place.

Assemble the ornament, using the second circle as the lining. Quilt around the appliqué pieces. Add a red hanging loop.

Cut a 2" by 20" strip of red fabric. Fold the strip in half lengthwise with the right sides together, and stitch ¼" from the edge, leaving a 3" opening at the center. Stitch across the ends diagonally *(Fig. 4)*. Turn the strip right side out; turn in the raw edges and slip-stitch. Tie the strip into a bow and tack it to the front of the ornament at the base of the hanging loop. Tack the streamers to the sides of the ornament so that they do not droop.

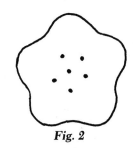

Fig. 2

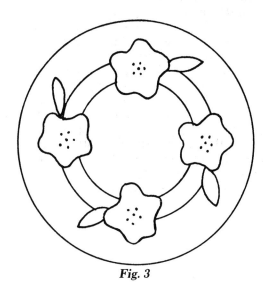

Fig. 3

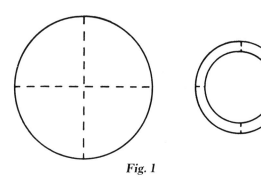

Fig. 1

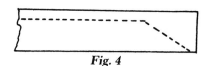

Fig. 4

Templates for this ornament appear on Plate 14.

Dresden Plate Ornament

Approximately 5″ in diameter

Materials

Red and off-white fabric
6″ square of quilt batting
Red quilting thread

Number of Pieces to Cut

Template A   1 red
Template B   8 red, 8 off-white

▨ Red

☐ Off-white

To Make

Alternating colors, sew 4 B wedges together along the long edges, being very careful to stop exactly on the seam line at the wider end. This forms one quarter of the circle *(Fig. 1)*. Repeat to form three more quarters. Sew the quarters together in pairs to form half-circles *(Fig. 2);* then sew the halves together to complete the circle *(Fig. 3).* then sew the halves together to complete the circle *(Fig. 3).* There will be a hole in the center of the circle.

Cut a 6″ diameter circle of muslin for the lining. Baste batting to the wrong side of the lining. Center the patched circle, wrong side up, on top of the lining; pin securely. Stitch around the outer edge of the patched circle on the seam line, pivoting the stitching at the corners and the points. Trim the edges of the lining even with the edges of the ornament, trimming the points of the wedges and clipping the inner corners of the lining. Trim the batting close to the stitching. Turn the piece right side out through the center hole. Appliqué the red A circle over the opening. Quilt around the center circle and along the seam lines of the wedges.

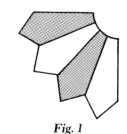

Fig. 1

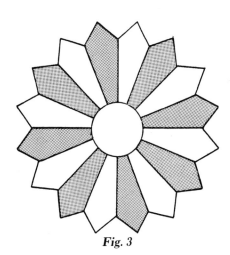

Fig. 2

Fig. 3

Templates for this ornament appear on Plate 15.

North Carolina Lily Ornament

Approximately 5″ by 5¾″

Materials

Red and off-white fabric
6½″ square of quilt batting
Red embroidery floss
Red and off-white sewing thread
Off-white quilting thread

Number of Pieces to Cut

Template A	6 red, 6 off-white
Template B	3 red
Template C	1 red
Template D	1 red

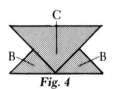

Red   Off-white

To Make

Sew each red A petal to an off-white A petal along one edge as in *Fig. 1*. Sew the joined petals together in pairs to form the three lilies *(Fig. 2)*. Sew the long diagonal edge of a B triangle to the long straight edge of one of the lilies *(Fig. 3)*. Sew a small B triangle to either side of the point of the large C triangle to form the basket *(Fig. 4)*. Cut a 5½″ by 6¼″ rectangle from off-white fabric. Pin the lilies, the stem *(Template D)* and the basket to this rectangle following *Fig. 5*. Cut a 1″ by 4″ strip of red. Fold the long raw edges to the center, then fold the strip in half lengthwise. Slip-stitch the edges together. Fold this strip to make a loop and insert the raw ends between the center petals of the top lily *(Fig. 6)*. Appliqué the pieces in place, attaching the loop as you sew. With red embroidery floss, work outline stitch along the outer edges of the white appliqué pieces.

Assemble the ornament; quilt along the seam lines.

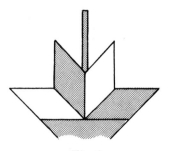

Fig. 4

Fig. 1

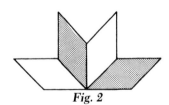

Fig. 2

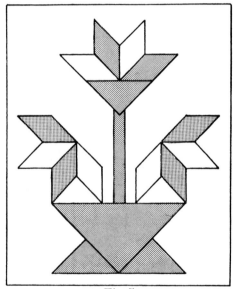

Fig. 5

Fig. 3

Fig. 6

Templates for this ornament appear on Plate 15.

Ozark Diamond Ornament

Approximately 5½″ by 6½″

Materials

Red and off-white fabric
6½″ square of quilt batting
Off-white sewing thread
Off-white quilting thread

Number of Pieces to Cut

Template A   1 red
Template B   18 off-white
Template C   12 red
Template D   6 off-white

 Red   ☐ Off-white

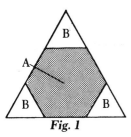

Fig. 1

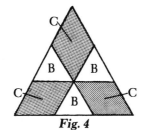

Fig. 2

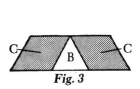

Fig. 3

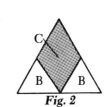

Fig. 4

To Make

Sew three B triangles to alternate edges of the A hexagon to form the center *(Fig. 1)*. Sew two B triangles to adjacent edges of a C diamond to form a triangle *(Fig. 2)*. Sew two C diamonds to two sides of a B triangle to form a strip *(Fig. 3);* sew the strip to the lower edge of the triangle just made to form a larger triangle *(Fig. 4)*. Repeat to form two more triangles. Sew these three triangles to the edges of the center *(Fig. 5)*. Make a triangle as in *Fig. 2* and sew a D diamond to two of the sides *(Fig. 6)*. Make two more units like this. Sew one of these units to each edge of the large center unit *(Fig. 7)*.

Assemble the ornament, adding a red hanging loop. Quilt around the outer edge of the star and around the center hexagon.

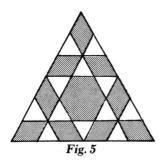

Fig. 5

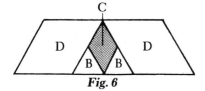

Fig. 6

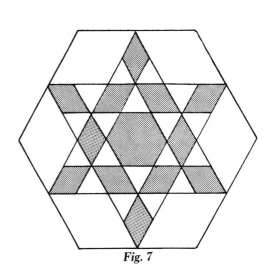

Fig. 7

Templates for this ornament appear on Plate 15.

Maple Leaf Ornament

Approximately 5" square

Materials

Red and off-white fabric
5" square of quilt batting
Red and off-white sewing thread
Red quilting thread

Number of Pieces to Cut

Template A   13 red, 20 off-white
Template B   16 red, 16 off-white

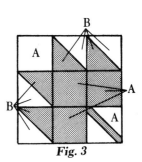

☐ Red

☐ Off-white

To Make

Trace the pieces to the fabric, but do not cut the off-white A squares yet. Cut a ⅜" by 2" strip of red fabric. Center this strip diagonally across one off-white A square; pin to hold. Appliqué the strip in place, using the tip of the needle to turn under ⅛" on the long edges. This forms the stem of the maple leaf *(Fig. 1)*. Repeat with three more off-white A squares. Cut out the squares, trimming the ends of the strips even with the edges of the squares. Sew red B triangles to off-white B triangles along the diagonal edge to form squares *(Fig. 2)*. Make four maple leaf blocks following *Fig. 3*, first sewing the patches together in horizontal rows, then joining the rows. Join remaining off-white A squares in groups of three, forming four strips. Sew a maple leaf block to each side of one of these strips, having the stems meeting the strip at the lower edge *(Fig. 4)*. Join the remaining maple leaf blocks to a second off-white strip in the same manner. Join the other two off-white strips to either side of the remaining red A square. Sew the blocks to this strip so that the stems touch the center red square *(Fig. 5)*.

Assemble the ornament and quilt around each maple leaf.

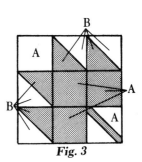

Fig. 3

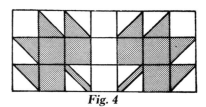

Fig. 4

Fig. 1

Fig. 2

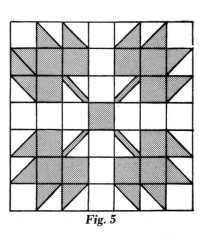

Fig. 5

Templates for this ornament appear on Plate 16.

Tulip Basket Ornament

Approximately 4½" by 5½"

Materials

Red and off-white fabric
Red embroidery floss
Red and off-white sewing thread
Off-white quilting thread

Number of Pieces to Cut

Template A	2 red, 2 off-white
Template B	1 red
Template C	2 red

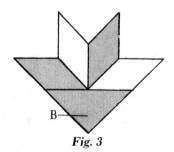
Red

Off-white

To Make

Sew each red A petal to a white A petal along one edge as in *Fig. 1*. Sew the two pairs together to form the tulip *(Fig. 2)*. Sew the long straight edge of the tulip to the long diagonal edge of the B basket triangle *(Fig. 3)*. Sew the two small C triangles to either side of the point of the B triangle to form the base *(Fig. 4)*. Cut a 1″ by 4″ strip of red. Fold the long raw edges to the center, then fold the strip in half lengthwise. Slip-stitch the edges together. Fold this strip to make a loop and sew the raw ends to the wrong side of the tulip piece between the center two petals *(Fig. 5)*. Cut a 5″ by 6″ rectangle from off-white fabric. Center the tulip basket on the rectangle; appliqué in place, leaving the loop free. With red floss, work outline stitch along the outer edge of the white tulip petals.

Assemble the ornament. Quilt along the seam lines.

Fig. 1

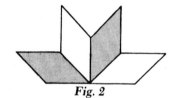

Fig. 2

Fig. 3

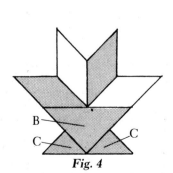

Fig. 4

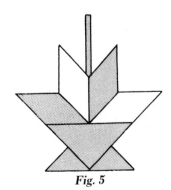

Fig. 5

Templates for this ornament appear on Plate 16.

Little Beech Tree Ornament

Approximately 5″ square

Materials

Red and off-white fabric
5″ square of batting
Red and off-white sewing thread
Red quilting thread

Number of Pieces to Cut

Template A	1 red
Template B	1 off-white
Template C	20 red, 24 off-white
Template D	8 red
Template E	1 off-white

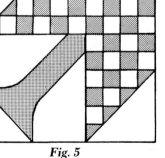

Red

Off-white

To Make

Appliqué the tree trunk *(Template A)* to the large off-white B square as in *Fig. 1.* Join C squares and D triangles as in *Fig. 2,* first joining them in rows, then sewing the rows together. Sew an E triangle to the diagonal edge of this piece to form a rectangle. Sew this rectangle to one side edge of the appliquéd square as in *Fig. 3.* Sew the remaining C squares and D triangles together as in *Fig. 4;* sew the other E triangle to the diagonal edge to make a rectangle. Sew this piece to the edge of the previously joined pieces following *Fig. 5.*

   Assemble the ornament, adding a red hanging loop at the top point of the tree. Quilt along the outer edges of the tree.

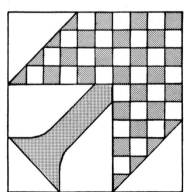

Fig. 3

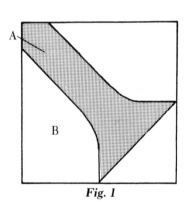

Fig. 1

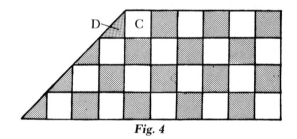

Fig. 4

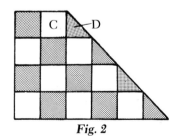

Fig. 2

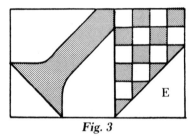

Fig. 5

Templates for this ornament appear on Plate 16.

Quilted Christmas Stockings

Heel Appliqué

Toe Appliqué

Berry
Appliqué

Template A

Holly Leaf Appliqué

Top of Stocking

Join to center of stocking on Plate 2,
matching small numbers

1

2

Plate 1

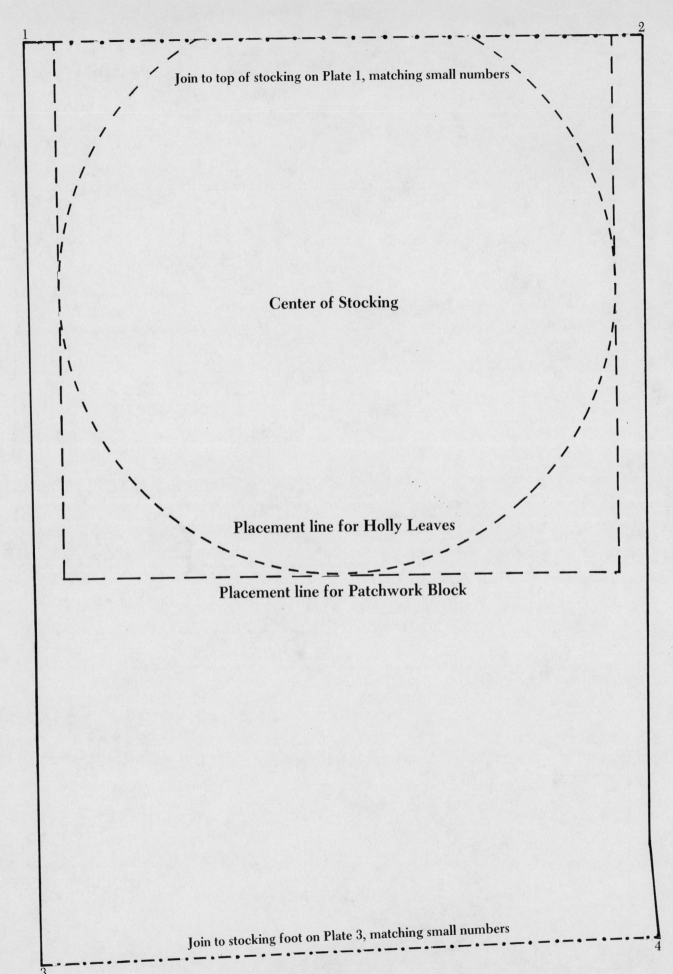

1   2

Join to top of stocking on Plate 1, matching small numbers

Center of Stocking

Placement line for Holly Leaves

Placement line for Patchwork Block

Join to stocking foot on Plate 3, matching small numbers

3   4

Plate 2

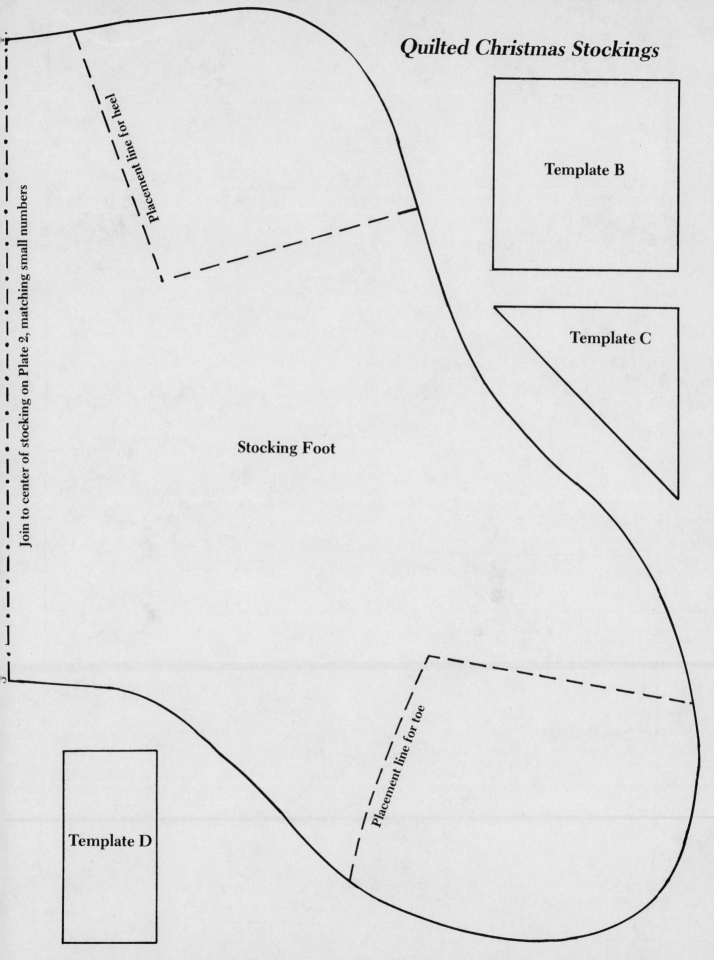

Quilted Christmas Stockings

Template B

Template C

Placement line for heel

Join to center of stocking on Plate 2, matching small numbers

Stocking Foot

Placement line for toe

Template D

Plate 3

Christmas Tree Wall Quilt

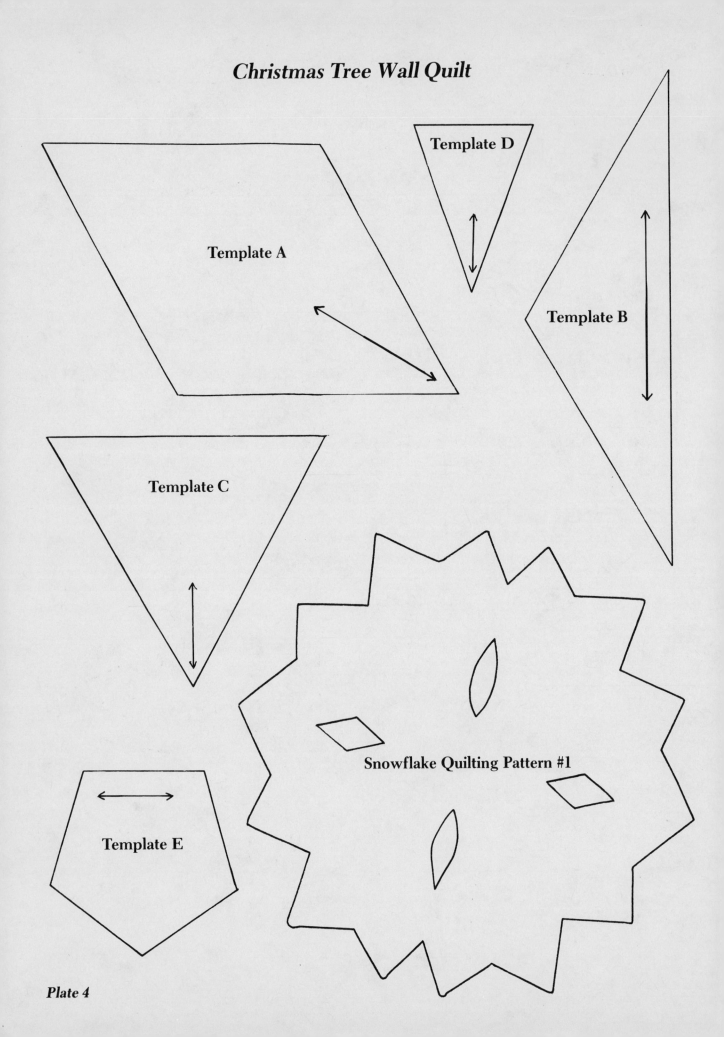

Template D

Template A

Template B

Template C

Snowflake Quilting Pattern #1

Template E

Plate 4

Christmas Tree Wall Quilt

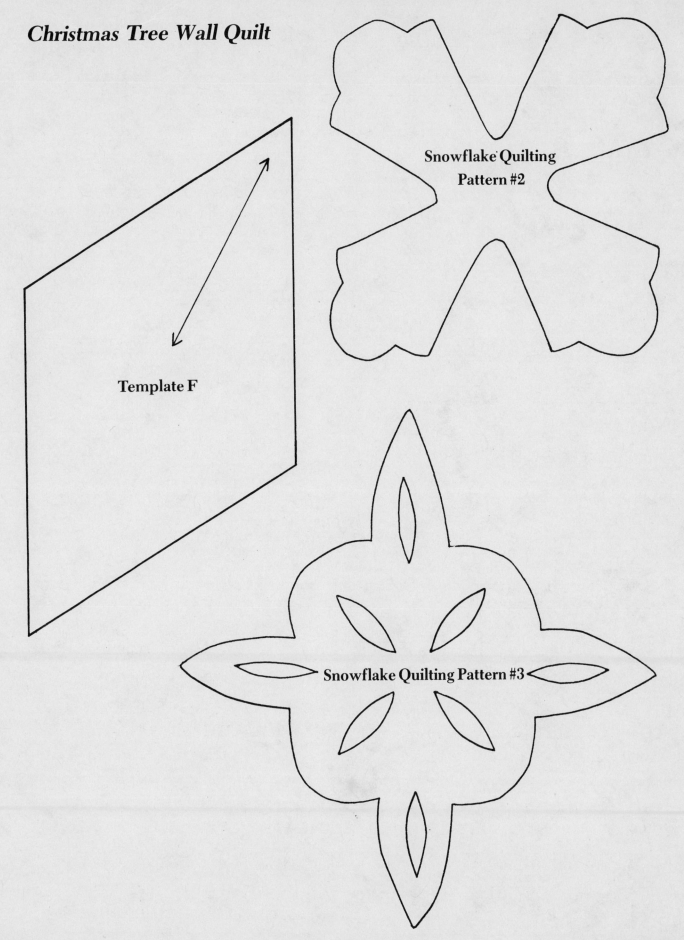

Template F

Snowflake Quilting Pattern #2

Snowflake Quilting Pattern #3

Plate 5

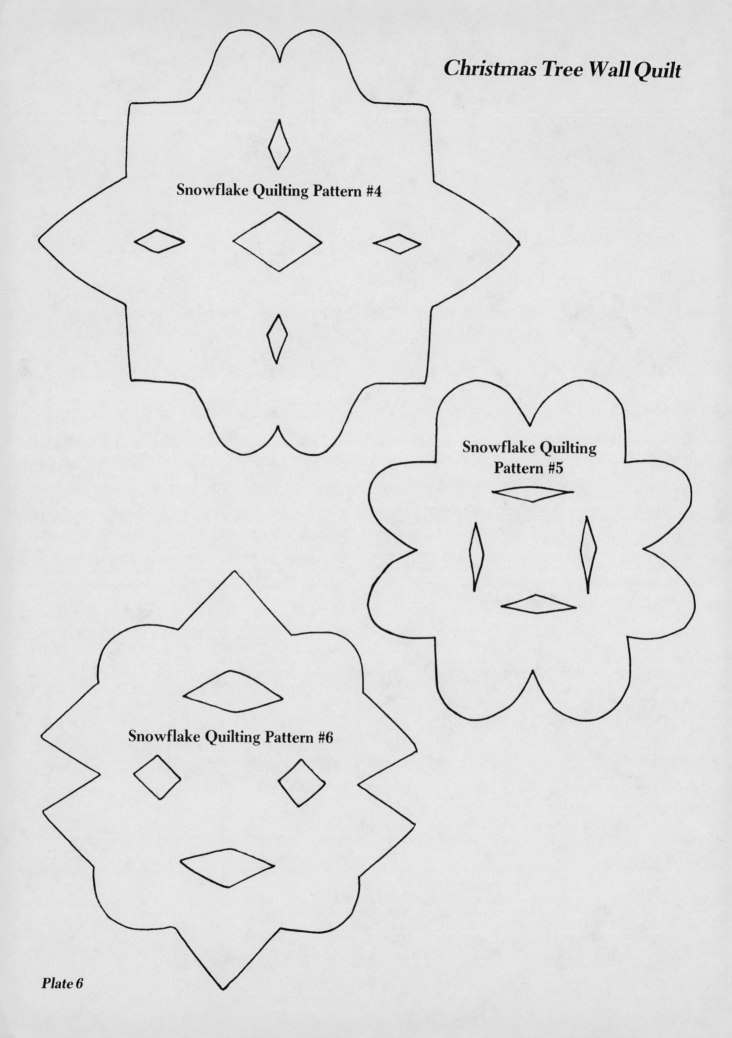

Christmas Tree Wall Quilt

Snowflake Quilting Pattern #4

Snowflake Quilting
Pattern #5

Snowflake Quilting Pattern #6

Plate 6

Log Cabin Tree Skirt

Template C

Template A

Template B

Template G

Template F

Template E

Template D

Plate 7

Log Cabin Tree Skirt

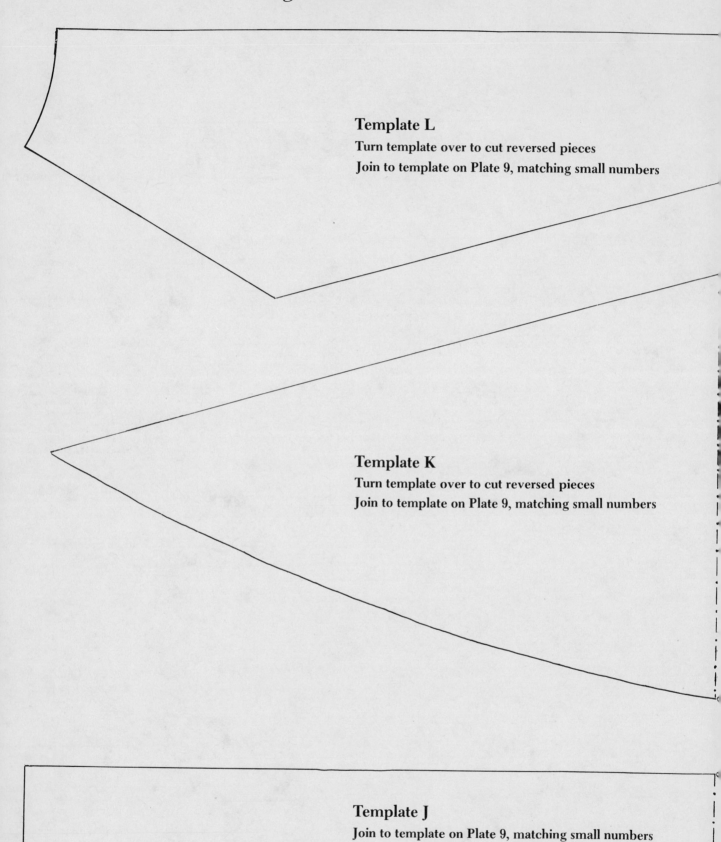

Template L

Turn template over to cut reversed pieces

Join to template on Plate 9, matching small numbers

Template K

Turn template over to cut reversed pieces

Join to template on Plate 9, matching small numbers

Template J

Join to template on Plate 9, matching small numbers

Plate 8

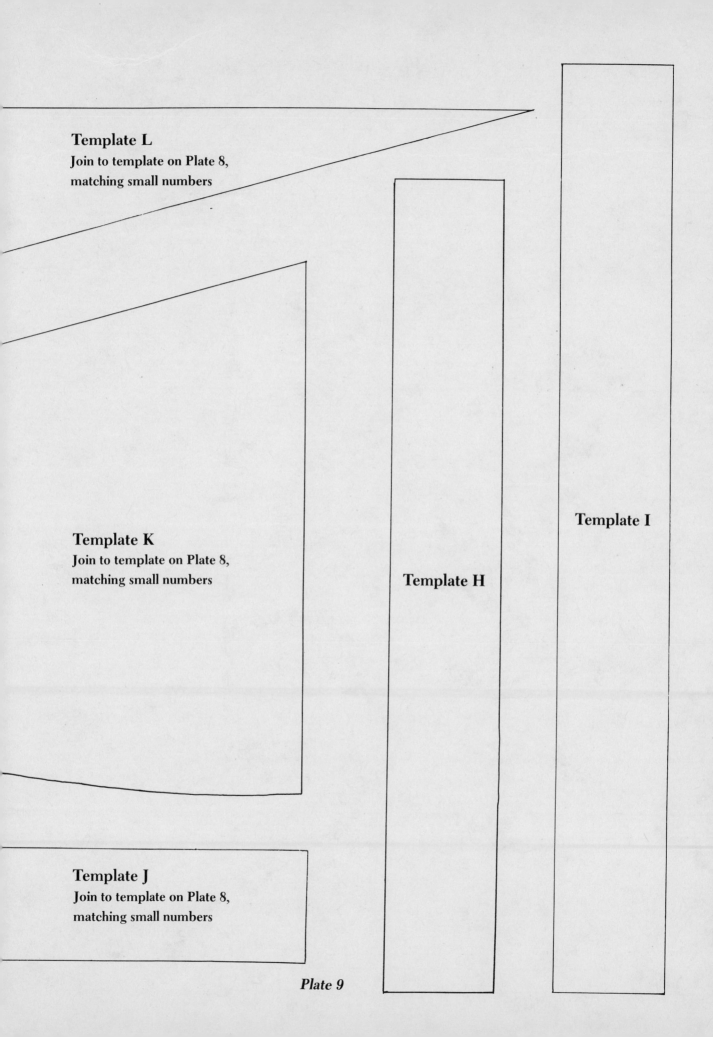

Template L
Join to template on Plate 8,
matching small numbers

Template I

Template K
Join to template on Plate 8,
matching small numbers

Template H

Template J
Join to template on Plate 8,
matching small numbers

Plate 9

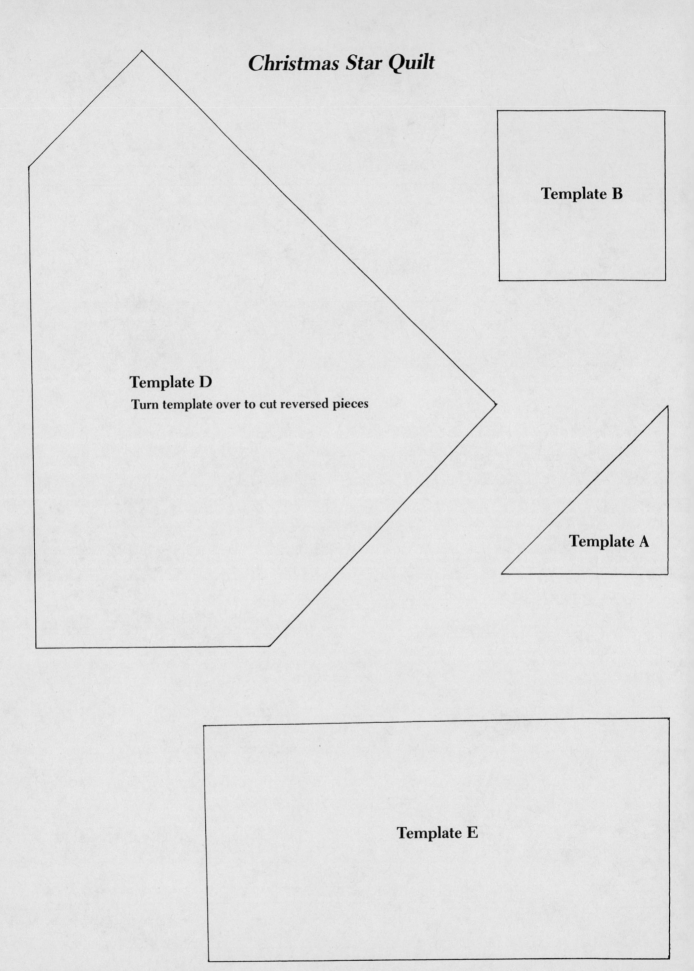

Christmas Star Quilt

Template B

Template D

Turn template over to cut reversed pieces

Template A

Template E

Plate 10

Christmas Star Quilt

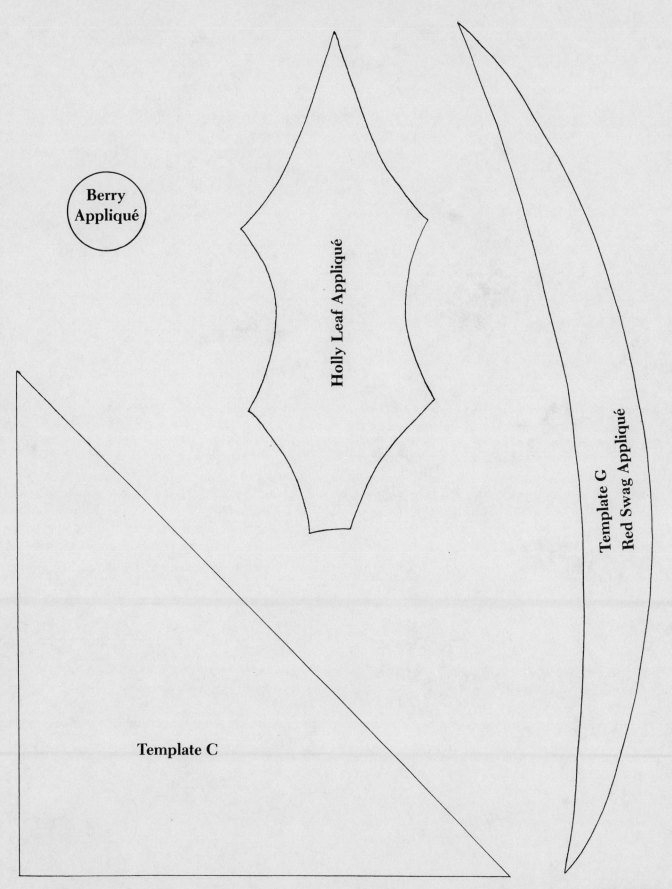

Berry Appliqué

Holly Leaf Appliqué

Template G
Red Swag Appliqué

Template C

Plate 11

Christmas Star Quilt

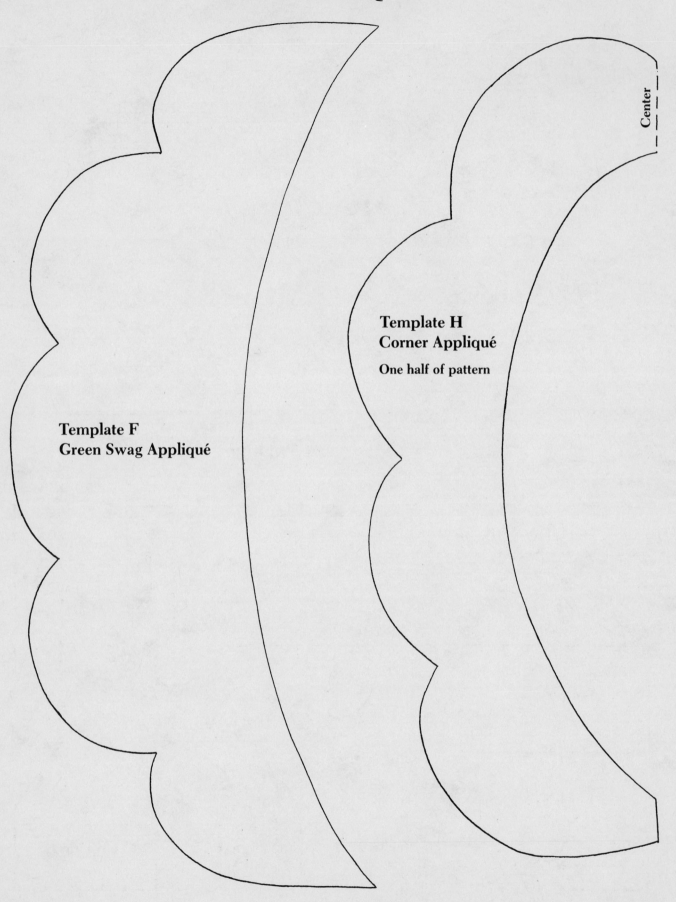

Center

**Template H
Corner Appliqué**

One half of pattern

**Template F
Green Swag Appliqué**

Plate 12

Holly Berry Wreath

Berry

Leaf

Schoolhouse Ornament

Template D

Template C

Template G

Template A

Template F

Template E

Template H

Template B

Turn template over to cut second piece

Template K

Template I

Template J

Plate 13

Star Ornament

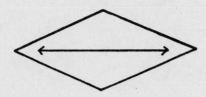

Grandmother's Flower Garden Ornament

Primrose Ornament

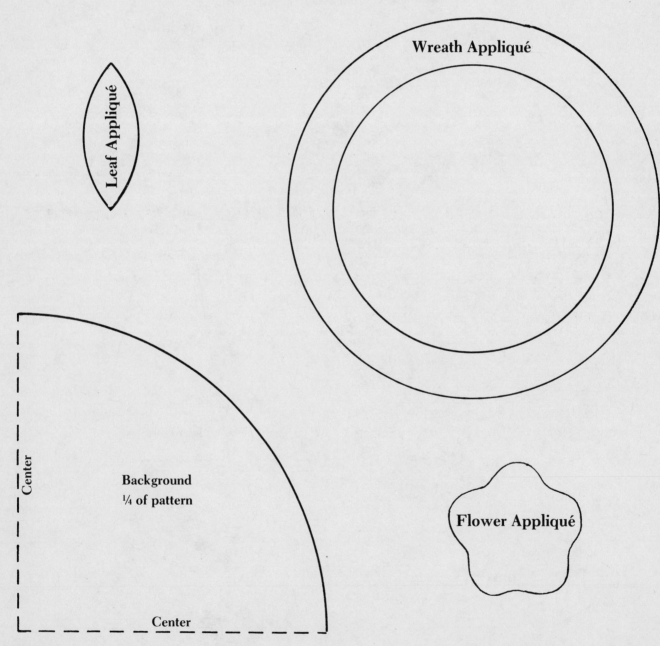

Leaf Appliqué

Wreath Appliqué

Center

Background
¼ of pattern

Center

Flower Appliqué

Plate 14

Dresden Plate Ornament

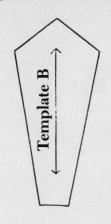

North Carolina Lily Ornament

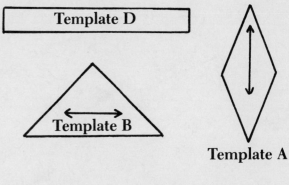

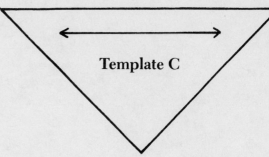

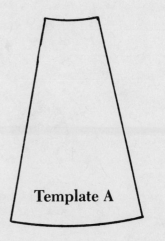

Ozark Diamond Ornament

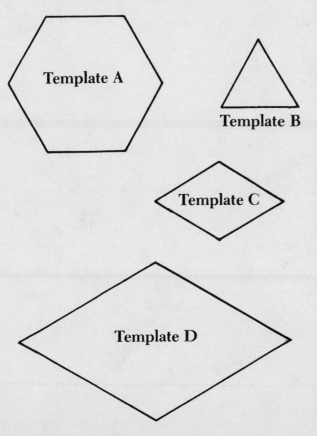

Grandmother's Fan Ornament

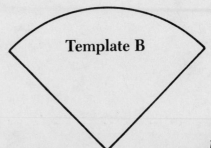

Plate 15

Maple Leaf Ornament

Template A

Template B

Tulip Basket Ornament

Template C

Template B

Template A

Little Beech Tree Ornament

Template E

Template C

Template D

Tree Appliqué

Template A

Template B

Plate 16